Right Side Up

The Proven Formula for Turning Your Bottom Producers into Your Top Performers

By Floyd Wickman

The Ten Lessons Every Leader Needs to Know...

Introduction

Right Side Up
June 2014

People often ask me how I have been able to turn so many bottom producing agents into top producing agents. The reason is empathy. I used to be one of those bottom producers. It wasn't until I found a new boss who showed me the ropes and literally made me responsible for my success that things turned around for me.

I've been sharing the concepts in this book with brokers and owners all around the country with great success. Too often leaders and managers bypass working with their bottom half because of the time and energy they think it will take up.

What follows is the transcript where I show brokers exactly how to turn their company right side up by turning their bottom half producers into their top half. The best part is how little time and energy it requires, and little or no financial investment.

Enjoy the book with my compliments.

I hope it opens your eyes to a new way of thinking - that the future growth of your company can be from within, and that it encourages you to lead your bottom to the top - The Wickman Way.

To Your Success!

Floyd Wickman

Right Side Up!

Dean: Hi, this is Dean Jackson and today I'm here with Floyd Wickman and I'm very excited because we're going to talk about all the experiences that Floyd's had in turning real estate companies right side up, so welcome Floyd.

Floyd: Thank you Dean, great to be here.

Dean: Well, I'm excited to hear this whole process, I know you've got a lot to share and you've had a pretty extensive background in helping companies turn their operations right side up, what do you mean by that?

Floyd: Well, I mean basically the most money that's lost by a company is in the bottom half of production, their agents in the bottom half of production. When a company can build on that and make the bottom half twice as productive, the whole organization goes up.

Dean: That's what you mean by turning right side up.

Floyd: Exactly.

How Real Estate Companies Differ?

Dean: Perfect, let's start out, I know you're saying that there are different types of companies that you see and there's going to be different types of people who are reading this, so what are the different kinds of companies that you've seen in all your experience there.

Floyd: Well, basically I see three types of companies. For lack of a better term, we'll call them A, B and C, or good, better and best. All companies are good and have their strengths and have their weaknesses. When I say A, B and C, we'll say A might be a company with a very small staff of agents. They might be light years from their market share potential. B might the larger staff of agents in a company and the company is substantially away from their full market share potential. Then of course, the C might be the more productive and successful company and that's the large staff of agents at or near their market share potential.

The reason I even see them that way is if I have a role in life, it's to help the A's become B's, the B's become C's and then help the C's prevent doing the wrong thing, so they don't end up a B. There's my focus in life. Put another way, I help the good become better, the better become the best and the best stay that way.

Why Do Real Estate Companies Under-Achieve?

Dean: You find now that over all of these years that all companies kind of fall into those categories. That makes sense because it is the large companies that tend to have the biggest market share and in every market you see, a company kind of dominates the market.

Floyd: Exactly and the question is, are they at their true potential for the number of agents they have and the number of leadership and offices they have. That's what I look at. Whenever I see a company, when I step into a company and analyze it and the broker is saying to me, "Help me get more production from my agents, help me get more listings and more sales, whatever the case may be." The first thing I like to do is take a look at the foundation of the company and I look for some common cracks in the foundation. Actually, there are five of them that I think need to be talked about and shored up if the company is going to grow to its full potential.

An example Dean, might be the first common crack, what I refer to as an upside down organizational chart and literally when I stand in front of an audience, I'll take a chart, where it says broker and below that is manager and then sales associates, below that and I'll actually turn it upside down over my head and I'll ask "How many of you know a company, where leadership is actually working every day, working their butts off, day and night to do everything that those agents want them to do." That's a little bit out of balance and I remind you of the story of the real estate broker whose son said, "Hey mom, how come dad has to come home late every single night and then when he comes home, he has all this work to do at home?" Mom says, "Well, you know, he can't get all this work done during the day." His son said, "Why don't they put him in a slower group?"

Of course, it isn't that. It's the amount of tasks that brokers and managers take on that keep them so busy and more times than not, it's doing things for the agents that the agents could and should be doing for themselves or at the very least together.

The second common crack I see Dean is what I call half of a job description. Whether it's the broker, president or CEO of a company, depending on the size of the company, maybe there are a couple of managers managing this staff of agents.

The boss says to the manager, "Okay, here's your responsibility. I want you to increase production by X%, I want you to add X number of agents to the base; I want you to increase our profit by this margin etc., etc., that's your responsibility. Oh and by the way, if you need anything, check with me first, I don't want you firing anybody and I want to do all the meetings. Simply put if a person is responsible to get the job done but can't make the decisions he has 1/2 of a job description, the responsibility without the authority. You're never going to get the full potential out of that manager. It won't happen. You have to establish the guidelines of course but certain authorities you have to give to them or they can't do the job to its fullest.

Dean: That makes a lot of sense.

Floyd: It is way too common and sometimes I'm able to get the leaders to take another look at some of these areas and it certainly helps.

There's a third area, common crack, that I see with some companies and that's low or no standards. One broker in Texas said, "Floyd, my people wouldn't live up to my standards." I said, "Well, what did you do?" He said, "I lowered them." Of course that isn't the answer. The answer is if you establish certain standards, whatever those standards might happen to be that means it's the stable datum, it's the bottom line and if you don't enforce standards, then nobody is going to follow standards. It's that simple. So, I always like to see what the standards are in the company. What is the expectation and requirement to be an agent here at this company? In other words, if I were an agent hired into a company, I would want to know what the core values are here in your company and the reason I want to know that is I want to know within what guidelines you expect me to operate. If you know about the Floyd Wickman Team, I'm sure you've seen this somewhere, we've got several core values, one being to live by the get by giving philosophy and one of them is to always do what we say we'll do, sometimes more, never less. What are our core values? Hire people that accept the core values and you let people go if they don't follow the core values. It's that simple.

The fourth crack that I look for is obsolete management style, Dean. When I say obsolete, I mean, there are three styles of management the "X" the "O" and "X" disguised as an "O".

For example let's take the X style of management. That's the "tell" and of course we know that the tell method of management became obsolete over the years but there are some brokers that are still trying to manage their people by not letting the people do any thinking.

Then, there's the second type of management style and that is what I call the "show and hope"; the "O"-style method, showing them what to do and hope to God that they do it. Now, we also know that doesn't work. So when we look at these and, say, "Okay, now what is the secret today, if I can't manager them with the X style, you don't want me to manage them with the O style, which style do I need?"

I say, Use that X disguised as an O. I call that team management and what I mean by team management is participation and common goals and core values.

That's the way to have team management, participation, common goals, common core values and then oftentimes it's treating the people in the lowest part of production one way, as a team perhaps and treating the people in the top part as a separate team because each has different goals and skills. It's very possible to have three separate teams in an office. I hate to use the word team because it's so misconstrued. I'm not talking about having a team leader and I'm not talking about all march as a band, I am talking a number of people working toward a common cause.

Then, finally the fifth common crack in the foundation I look for is a weaknesses in any of the jobs of the manager. Managers have five jobs: recruit, train, direct, motivate and upgrade.

Although everyone knows that, what a lot of people don't realize is these are links in a chain and the effect of this on that company is as strong or as weak as the weakest link. That's one of the things that I talk with brokers about and I really want to help them solidify these links because it's a great way to help a company achieve permanence.

The Role Leadership Plays in a Real Estate Company's Success...

Dean: Do you think that when people are shown these cracks in their foundation, do you think that a lot of the reason why they don't have standards or they're trying an obsolete management style, is it fear or is it just apathy, what's been your kind of experience when you see this. This all sounds very clear and do people recognize them when you point them out to them?

Floyd: Absolutely, they do and yes, in other words that is common; fear, apathy, even not knowing exactly how to do it without rubbing their agents the wrong way. That's where relationship comes in.

When my trainers or I go in to a company with my training program, training the agents the Wickman Way, the students are not my client, the company is my client. The students happen to be components of that company and my role is to help the company earn more by helping the agents produce more. It's about that simple. What happens when we go in and we begin this, we begin a relationship with a company. Sometimes it takes months and we don't mind that. Sometimes, it takes six months to help a company get these cracks in the foundation shored up.

All of my trainers are experts at helping companies do these sorts of things. If we're going to train your agents, we consider ourselves part of your leadership team.

Dean: Oh that's great and the more I'm thinking about it as you're describing these things, it does come down to the leadership role, doesn't it?

Floyd: Absolutely, the leadership is the face of the company and when we say the face of the company, we're talking about the person that is the founder in many cases or the ultimate leader. That person has to have certain standards, methods, attitudes and sometimes they're good and sometimes they're bad. I'll tell you what, I have a great deal of admiration and respect for real estate brokers and managers because they work harder today than they ever have. But they don't have to work quite as hard for production to increase if they patch up some of these cracks. It's so easy for me after all these years to say, "Okay, these are the common cracks and these are the types of companies, but the important aspect of this is normality. I ask the management group, "How many of you are normal, how many reading this are normal?"

I ask them to show their hands and sure, if I am with a group and I say, I'm about to talk about your company, your office, your situation and I'm going to talk about your agents; "Ron the Rebel," "Know-It-All Nellie," "Carlos the Con Man," "Tina the Time Stealer" and I've never been in your office. If you are normal, you've got to ask yourself this question, "How does he know?" What I wanted to do, in this part of this book, I want to earn a little right to pass on tips and techniques by taking you back to this unique perspective that I have into the real estate business. I probably have the most unique perspective in the business of any trainer or training company on the circuit today. I don't mean the best necessarily and I don't mean the only one necessarily but I do mean the most unique perspective.

How Floyd Turned His Production Right Side Up...

I've seen this business from every angle and what I mean by that is, I came into real estate many years ago, after almost 10 years in the Navy and a ninth-grade education. When I came into this real estate business I was the hungriest agent in the whole state. I was so proud to be able to call myself a real estate agent. I could wear a suit and tie and not get blisters on my hands, like my uncles and dad, "Wow, I could really do this." I worked and I worked seven days a week, 12 hours a day. Over the first 11 and half months, I produced, I don't mean to brag, five sales and two fell through. That's seven days a week, 12 hours a day.

Well, there was an interesting lesson I learned. You know what lessons are Dean, when you get lessons from somebody; those aren't the how- to's. When you get a lesson, you think, "Knowing this lesson, I've got to learn how to use this lesson to my benefit." The experience of being a failing salesman for so long taught me some lessons. Then, I met a new broker. His style was to the right of "Attila the Hun". The type of guy when he dies, I want his heart. I don't want him to die. But his heart was just never used. Just kidding. Anyhow, he grabbed me, day one, he said, "Wickman, if you are going to work here, you're going to be a million-dollar producer."

Now, get the picture, the average sale price at that time was $11,400 for the whole house, not the deposit. I'd already been working seven days a week, 12 hours a day, I made five sales and two fell through. He said I was going to go from three to over 90 and here I am the same guy. Well, you know, I did make the million dollar club again and again and again. I averaged 86 listings a year for the next seven and a half years. The reason I even say that is I was the same guy, so I learned some lessons there that made me what I am today and I'm able to pass on to my clients and my trainers.

Then I said, "To heck with this, I want to make all the money," so I wanted to be a manager. This is when an audience will normally laugh because nobody gets into management for the money. They get into management because, look, if they're not running the parade, they're not even going to go to watch the parade. They just have to be the leader.

I was that sort and so I managed a staff of eight associates in Farmington Hills, Michigan, and when I say they collectively averaged 23 closings a month, those eight people for four consecutive years in suburban Michigan, most people say it's a lot of production. Well, they did do that and from that I learned valuable lessons that made me and my trainers what we are today. This wasn't just a fluke, I didn't sit at drawing boards, "Okay, I'm going to be a trainer and let me figure out everything I want to teach somebody." No, we oftentimes teach what we need the most. After four years of that I said, "I want to be a trainer."

I trained for a seven office chain and then I went as regional training director for a franchise and I became the national training director for the franchise. All of a sudden, working for franchise and independent companies, I'm all over North America and I'm teaching my stuff all over North America, by goodness, all of a sudden, I'm learning more lessons. Then finally, in 1979, I walked away from the corporate world and I said, "I have to do my thing, I just want to do what I want to do." I thought I was going to be a speaker, "Man, speakers are great, they fly you in first class and put you up in a nice hotel and you sell a bunch of product, get back on the plane first-class, go home, a wonderful way to make a buck."

But, it usually doesn't change anybody permanently. I was doing a talk in Sterling Heights, a suburban area of Detroit years ago. About 300 to 400 people were in the room and I'm teaching closing techniques but I could see in their eyes because of the economy, the sense of hopelessness. I said, "I know you're having a rough market right now gang, but let me tell you something, if you have the guts to do everything I tell you to do, and do everything I ask you to do, I'll train you for a year and won't charge you any money. I know that you can't control the economy but you can control your economy, I know that, I've lived it." I had 23 people and I put them through my very first program ever as a freelance trainer. I might have met with them once a week for 13 weeks. 13 weeks, I ran out of material. I said I would train them for a year; I don't have anything else to teach.

But, those 23 people in 91 days brought in 247 listings and 118 sales.

Dean: Wow.

Floyd: I know and the interesting thing was every single one of them was in the bottom 50% of production in their companies when they started. By the way, I have to let you in on a little secret, I even fibbed to them a little. I said, "Well, you all have to take an aptitude test." I said to each of them eyeball to eyeball, "Boy, your score came in, wow, did you score high; you are like a volcano, getting ready to erupt." It wasn't important what the test said, it's what they believed and for some reason they believed me, wow, was that something. Yeah, I learned some lessons there too.

The bottom line is that's how my spaced training program was created and today we've got well over 350,000 people who have completed the Floyd

Wickman Program, graduated from the multi-week program and the productivity is just short of amazing. Even though 82% were in the bottom half of production in their companies when they started the program, they averaged one transaction per person per week and 2.3 referrals generated per person per week. One year after graduation 65% ended up in the top half.

The Ten Lessons Every Leader Needs to Know

Lesson #1

Give Your People the Option to Fail and 70% Will Take That Option Every Time

Dean: I'm excited to hear all about your lessons that you learned and the journey.

Floyd: The first lesson Dean is that if you give people the option to fail, 70% will pick that option every time because it's a lot easier. If you really want to take responsibility for a person to be successful, take away the option, until they are successful. Then, let them fly.

Lesson #2

People Are as Good or as Bad as You Train or Allow Them to Be

Second lesson I learned is that our people are as good or as bad as we train or allow them to be. I mean those were things I learned as a failing salesman and then as a successful salesperson. All of a sudden, my new boss took away the option, I didn't have an option to fail. Then he made me learn to sell. I took a sales training program for 9 months called STI and learned for myself when you can sell anything ... you can sell anything.

Lesson #3

Listings Are the Name of the Game

Here's the next lesson I learned. All I want to do is have a lot of closings to make money and I didn't want to work so much anymore. He made sure I only worked five and a half days a week and I had learned this lesson that listings are the name of the game. Isn't that funny I would say that because every trainer in the world says that. I mean first time I ever heard that was Jerry Bresser many, many years ago listings are the name of the game. But you know what, sometimes the only way we realize that is when we live it, when we spend a year almost working our butts off trying to make sales and all of a sudden we find out that listings are the name of the game. When you can list, you can sell. When you could sell, it doesn't mean you can list. That's why I make my students learn to be a lister first.

Lesson #4
Build from the Bottom

The fourth lesson I learned is you build from the bottom. Just like I said at the outset, give me your bottom 50%, you give me the people that are experienced, maybe at least a year in real estate, they are in the bottom 50% of production, let me have those people because that's what I lived and that's what I do the best. I can get those people to average one transaction per person per week. An interesting truth Dean is that the bottom 50 pays the most to the company because the commission split that a company gets is greater at that level.

When they are not productive, you're losing money by what they're not doing and it compounds itself, mathematically I can't even figure how to say that.

Dean: The mathematics of that Floyd if you look at the agents who have already reached their production cap, where now they're on a higher split that the broker is now just getting a transaction fee or a smaller percentage of the transaction than the people in the bottom that's where they're still getting the bigger proportion of the commission on the transaction.

Floyd: The beautiful thing is these were lessons that I lived and learned and proved. You know that some trainers like to specialize in the top producers, but I think I can really help solve a problem for a company by focusing my energies on the bottom producers.

Lesson #5
Leadership Is a Chain of Events

The other lesson I learned was some things about solidifying those links in the chain. As I said earlier, management has five jobs, recruit, train, direct, motivate and upgrade and success is as strong or as weak as the weakest link. So sometimes I'll sit with a broker or a manager and I'll say, "Let's look at each link and if I could give you one piece of advice in each of those links, what advice would I give you, here it comes." "If I were to give you one piece of advice on recruiting, it's hire new people."

Dean: That's exactly what most recruiters do. They're focused on getting the top producers. If they can get a top producer, they feel like that's a big win.

Floyd: I don't disagree with that. But to focus, the energy has to be on finding the experienced agents who are not yet successful. Bringing people into the real estate business and helping those already in it to become the success they wanted to be when they first became licensed. I just finished coaching a company and working with their recruiter. We made huge strides with this recruiter who was doing all the wining and dining with the top producers in their area. I said, "Well first of all, you have to keep up that wining and dining, but you better spend a good portion of your day contacting the lower producing agents and interviewing new people, advertising for new people, getting face to face with new and lower producing experienced people because if all you're going to do is shoot for the top producing agents, you're never going to build your company to its full potential." That is because of the time and the money and the energy it takes to hire top agents....and that's because they are happy and already successful so if you can't show them how they can be happier and more successful, you're taking the path of most resistance.

Dean: Now, when you say new, are you talking specifically about people who are not yet in real estate, you're saying introduce people to the idea of a career in real estate and mold them from the ground up. That's what you're saying?

Floyd: Yeah that and focusing on people in license schools now and I know the attitude, I mean I've been wrestling with this for a long time. The attitude, "Gee Floyd, if I hire them, I have to train them."

Dean: Train them, right.

Floyd: Okay and I know that but you know what, not necessarily, that's what guys like me are here for, just bring them in, let us train them. That's the bottom line.

Dean: It seems like that's part of some company's recruiting strategy. Let's let them get started and there's always one or two companies in town that do have a lot of training and they'll say, "Well, let them go over there and get their training started and then we'll poach them when they're not happy with their split."

Floyd: Yeah, exactly and guess what, there are solutions to that. I mean in other words you can keep people longer if you check the cracks in the foundation of your company, but if money is somebody's only motivator, eventually they're going to move unless you give them all of it. I mean it's just the way of life and keep in mind, I said you have to spend your time attracting experienced agents, you have to spend time schmoozing them, sending letters, having lunch every now and then. You have to spend your time doing it, but the basic of the business of recruiting is interviewing, is being face-to-face with new people and helping others become more successful than they are with their existing company.

What happens is, I'm not even elaborating on much of the recruiting programs that I have done over the years, but for years, I did a program called Head Hogs and well over 1,000 companies have been through that and we focus on hiring new and experienced agents for many years and the bottom line is when your system works, where you're interviewing on a daily basis, new people for your business and you're farming, I guess that's a better word, experienced agents in your area, then you're going to get the highest results in your recruiting efforts, so that a percentage will be experienced and a larger percentage will be the new people.

Dean: Perfect.

Lesson #6

Inspect Not Expect

Floyd: When I go back to those links in the chain, I look at the second link, which is to train. I'm going to spell this out word for word, what is the one piece of advice I can give a broker or a manager on training new people and I say even when I'm with a live group, I'll say, "You write this down word for word, make them strong at the basics first." I say it to a group. I put a lot of thought into exactly those words. Make them means, give them the option to do it and they won't do it. Make them meaning, not just one, but all of them. Strong, strong means competent, confident and natural. At the basics and the most basic basic of this business is talking to prospects, nothing is more basic and you can even get more basic to build those muscles, use the phone. You're going to be face to face, you're going to get internet leads, but whatever it has to be, you've got to be using your voice.

Dean: Sure, the trend of course has certainly moved to online lead generation and people starting their search online, but ultimately it's going to come down to, at some point you're going to talk to people.

Floyd: Right, exactly, I was speaking on the West Coast just recently and I said to an audience, "Okay, let me give you the secret to handling internet inquiries, write this down." Tease them to talk the secret is get voice to voice. When I said, tease them to talk, everybody was sitting there like a deer in the headlights meaning, what do you do? Would you like to know the number one way to tease somebody Dean?

Dean: Yes, I would love to.

Floyd: I'll tell you later.

Dean: Wait, wait don't go.

Floyd: The bottom line is if you ever don't want to talk to somebody, you just keep sending them information and if you're going to put them in a drip campaign, make sure that somewhere in the drip campaign there is a P.S. that offers some kind of hook to get voice to voice.

So, make them stronger at the basics first, and then I look into their eyes and say to people, "Write this down, your people are more apt to do what you inspect than what you expect." If you're going to say to new people, and I think this is awfully important, if you're going to say to new people especially ones that you're training, "I want you to do this, this, this and this," but you don't have a way a week later of taking a look at what they did and what their results are. It's just a matter of numbers, looking at their numbers.

Bottom line is if you don't do that the second week, you say, "I want you to do this, this and this," they're not going to do it. It's funny, when I was a new trainer I was sitting in a lounge in Battle Creek, Michigan. That's where you speak when you're just new at this. Anyhow, I'm sitting at the Holiday Inn, in the lounge and two stools over from me, this guy was sitting there. After a little while, we started talking. I said, "Hey, how are you doing?" "Good", he said. We talked. I said, "What do you do for a living?" He said "I'm a teacher." I thought, "Wow, man, I'm one of those too, sort of." I said, "I'm a teacher myself. What do you teach?" He said, "I teach third grade. What do you teach?" I thought for a second, and I said, "Well, actually now that I think about it I do too." They're taller, some of them are bald and things like that but I do too.

Because if you say to kids, "I want you to do this" and you don't check up on them they're not going to do it the next week, even though you tell them. Because they know they're not going to be inspected. By the way, speaking of that the next link in the chain is to motivate. How do you motivate a person? Well, there is a basic way and that's to find out what they want and show them how they can get it. I think that's always a good way to help motivate, but you know what that doesn't always work. If I'm with a live group, I'll say, "Pretend we're best friends" and you say, "Hey, Floyd, how do I motivate a guy?" I'll say, "Okay, write this down." They get the pen out, and I say, "You can't."

What I mean by that is you can't motivate anybody to do anything unless at that moment in their life, they are ready, willing and able to be motivated. Now, by the same token, you can motivate a team fairly easily. If you got a dozen people that need motivation, form them into one team and you'll motivate the majority of them. People are funny; they will work harder, so their team wins. Then, they will win, so their family can be happier.

Then, the final thing is upgrade; it's the job of managers. Now, I usually spell that for an audience, F-I-R-E. Now, what I mean by that is some people go out of their way to hurt an office and what I mean by that is here, I'll say to a broker "Look, you have to get rid of Ben." Brokers would say, "Why?" "Well, you don't like him and he doesn't like you and actually the agents don't like him and he doesn't like the agents and guess what the customers don't like him, he doesn't like customers, you've got to get rid of this guy. It's like a plant, you walk in, your plant's starting to droop, you can sit and talk to it all you want, it is not going to come back until you cut off some of the dead branches and then the water will take effect. "The fertilizer will take effect."

Dean: Fertilizer.

Floyd: Yes, yes, exactly, oh boy and then brokers say, "Well, Floyd, who's going to cover their phone time?" They have different excuses why they don't want to let somebody go. "Theirs is full time, who's going to cover?" I said, "Well, you know, to be honest with you, you could close the office during their time and increase production, you shut off all the phones and production would probably go up."

Dean: I need to try this.

Floyd: What I try and look at is those links of the chain and I try and make sure that they're all solid, because the end result is as strong or as weak as the weakest link. The next item is numbers. One lesson I learned, what you can do with numbers, numbers solve all the problems. Numbers, when I coach people, Dean, all I want are their numbers. I want to see the numbers constantly. The numbers they give me, the contacts and the number of appointments and number of this, they give me all the categories. The first week, they give it to me; it doesn't say much, it gives us a little something to talk about. But if I get their numbers week after week after week after week for about six weeks, seven weeks, I know exactly the little tweak I have to do to dramatically increase that person's production. It's the ultimate way of helping somebody improve.

Dean: You can certainly tell a trend week after week. It's hard to make a movie from a snapshot, but when you see multiple numbers, you see the whole picture developing.

Floyd: Yeah and numbers take the emotion out of it. I ask the audience, "How many of you are married?"

Their hands go up and I say, "I don't know about

you, but have you ever gone through this crap?"

> "Do you want to go to the movies?"
> "I don't know, do you want to go the movies?"
> "I don't know."
> "Are you hungry?"
> "I don't know, are you hungry?"

In my home, we designed a number system, on a scale of one to 10, how hungry are you, "Well, I'm a seven, how about you?" "Well, I'm a five." "When you get to nine, I'll be a seven, we'll go." You see, it takes out all the emotion. "How are you doing Charlie?" "Oh pretty good." As a leader, what am I going to do with that? That's why in my programs, everything has to have numbers, and then I know everything I need to know, I don't have to be with them to know.

Lesson #7

The Higher the Standards, the Longer the Line to Get In

The next one is the higher the standards, the longer the line to get in. It's another lesson I learned. If a broker would say, "I don't want everybody working here, I only want dedicated hard working people that dress to the nines," there'd be a line to get in that place. For sure, you will attract new and more and better people.

Dean: That makes a lot of sense.

Lesson #8

Education without Application Is Worse than Worthless

Floyd: The eighth lesson and I learned this teaching for a franchise. Now, remember I wrote the programs. I trained trainers to train the programs, but we had to have a certain kind of a system of training, of getting the information across. But there's one thing I learned, which changed my whole life as a trainer and that is that education without application is worse than worthless because it takes time, money and energy and if they aren't applying it, what good is it, zero value. There's somebody who said, "Well, knowledge is power." Yeah, but I'll tell you what, knowledge without application or a skill is not power period. Knowledge can certainly help a person become more powerful.

Dean: There's a great book called *You Can't Teach a Kid to Ride a Bike at a Seminar.*

Floyd: I love it, isn't that the truth.

Dean: You can understand the theory of how to ride a bike, but you can't do it until you've had the experience or application of trying it.

Floyd: Absolutely, now the seminar to teach them how to help somebody ride a bike and then team them with an adult and then give them two hours to go out in the parking lot and practice and then come back, that seminar made a difference.

Dean: That's perfect.

Lesson #9

Your Area Is Not Different

Floyd: Yeah, the ninth lesson I learned Dean is that your area is not different, period. If we get the same results, my program I could tell you, it's like a science. Now, our average per person production during the program is 1.01 transactions per person per week currently. It's been that way for many years. They're averaging 2.3 referrals generated per person per week and been doing that for years. We get the same results in Tuscaloosa, Alabama, Miami, Florida, Los Angeles, Albuquerque, New Mexico, Boston, Massachusetts and in Vancouver, British Columbia. So there can't be an area that's different because selling is selling, people are people and what motivates people one place motivates them other places.

If my program works everywhere, then nobody can ever say our area is different. What is different is an average sale price, which would bring down the unit production a little bit or length of time on the market, current financial situation. When it comes to listing and selling real estate, it's all the same. I do business with somebody where 80% of the owners live out of state but it doesn't change the process of selling or the process of listing, it just doesn't change it.

Lesson #10

People Want and Need
Tough Love Leadership

Finally number 10, people want and need tough love leadership for a period of time. Now, isn't that funny and I can prove that because if a broker puts 100 agents in a room, we spend three hours with them and we say, "Look, we're going to charge you a fortune, you've got to do everything we tell you to do or three strikes and you're out of the program, we've got to wear these silly t-shirts, we recite affirmations, how many want in?" Almost half of the people in that room are going to walk up and sign up to pay a lot of money for them. They have somebody give them that tough love leadership for a period of time.

Dean: Wow, people are silently begging to be led, aren't they?

Floyd: Listen, people are drowning in a sea of information, yet they're thirstier for direction right now than they have ever been.

Dean: Wow, those are some pretty powerful lessons Floyd. You could see each one of them has come from an experience and varied experience and repeated experience since 1979. A lot of those were learned as you were turning yourself from a failing salesperson working hard, into a successful salesperson with the right guidance and direction into a manager and then a trainer and then helping agents all over the country, helping brokers help their agents all over the country, amazing.

Floyd: Yeah. That was well put, I mean it is. It's those lessons. People say, "Wow, everything I have accomplished." It was like climbing Mount Everest, but I'll tell you what, the lessons were the spikes that pulled me up one body length at a time if that's the case." We teach what we need the most.

How to Flip Your Company Right Side Up...

Floyd: Okay, well you know, I guess if there's a bottom-line lesson, it's how to change somebody permanently because a broker doesn't need me to do so if they can use these following five ingredients. Now, stick with me. When I first came into real estate, most training was Monday through Friday, nine to five, "Now go out and get successful." Now, of course we know that all that information people are learning is important but most of what they learn on Tuesday, they won't remember by Friday. We know that. That's what the experts tell us. I've got five basic components of my training that guarantee success.

Dean: I'd like to hear.

Floyd: Okay, first of all spaced training; I conduct seven sessions, one each week with these people and we spend from 9:30 to 3:30 and I teach them everything they need to know to go further. Then they have to go, apply themselves. Then they come back and I give them very specific assignments, send them off, they have to apply themselves and when they come back, I don't joke when I say this, I teach them what they wished they would have had last week. You talk about opening a mind, I say this week, "You go out and you make X number of calls, you call for X number of time and come on and I'll see you next week." Then, I teach them how to turn those calls into appointments and handle the obstacles. Then, each week, when I teach them what they wished they would have had last week, you've got to see their faces. I mean I'm like a proud father watching my son or daughter have this revelation, like, that's what everybody wants for their kids. That's what I want for my students.

But if I gave it all to them seven days in a row, it wouldn't mean anything period, unless I could get them to apply themselves for the next six weeks or so.

The second ingredient is mandatory activity. Well, for some people their best might be making one contact and that's on Facebook. You got to learn that skill too. I do say to people, I just made that comment that agents if they're not using Facebook and they don't have skill, they're never going to make it in this business. If they are using Facebook and they don't have the skills, to list and sell, voice to voice, face to face, then they're never going to be at their full potential. If they can sell but they're not using Facebook, they won't be at their full potential and it's when they put the two together that empowers them to be consistently successful.

Third ingredient is accountability; again people are more apt to do what you inspect than what you expect. I want to know that they did that assignment. We invite brokers and managers into the classes and many times if it's a multiple office company, they'll have their managers be a whole separate team and focus their energies on recruiting. How many interviews did you have? How many conversations? We give them those assignments but if they don't do the assignment, we give them a "strike". They know it in advance. They know if they get three strikes, we're going to put them out of the program and they don't get a refund. I think that's what makes the program successful and it's also something that most companies can't do within. There needs to be this outsider coming in and saying, "Here are the rules," for it to be really effective.

The fourth ingredient of my program is role playing. I saw this on a milk carton one time, made me a better teacher. I don't remember what the context was, it said, "I hear and I forget, I see and I remember, I do and I understand." Most of the dialogues, these people learn at least 120 dialogues over this period of time, but they don't just hear them, they don't just see them, they role play them. The more they role play, the more they understand and the better the odds they're going to use it in a tough situation. When you really understand something, you can really be yourself.

The last ingredient is teamwork. Of course everybody has heard teamwork makes the dream work. I like to tell people, "Look we don't have it all together, but together we have it all, Together we can accomplish more." If there are two teams in a class and they compete against each other that's a big part of production. When you look at each of the five components of my program as an acronym, S.M.A.R.T, combined these are the SMART way to build skills and production... Take that person and make that person independent of you and not dependent on you, which should be the ultimate goal of every teacher and trainer anywhere. I'd like to answer the question that comes up, is this program a fit for you? But, first, I want to mention five very recent programs. The only reason I say this is when you've been around a long time, they sort of think "Well, you're old fashioned." Like McDonald's? Are they old fashioned?

Dean: Exactly.

How Effective Is the Program?

Floyd: Listen, everybody has to change with the times, but not always in major ways. You take McDonald's, now they've got their Wi-Fi and they're now working on specializing in coffee as much as they do hamburgers. But they're still there and the hamburgers are the same. In my business, I used to focus my energies on cold calling, but things change. Now, I have to use the same skills but calling for referrals or for sale by owners or expireds. Here's an example, take my last five programs, RE/MAX of New Jersey had 27 people graduate the program recently with my trainer Jack Alia and 27 people in 42 days brought in 107 listings, 156 sales. Their per-person production was 1.63 transactions per person per week.

There's a large, successful independent company in New England, The Jack Conway Company, 48 of their people took the program with my trainer

Sheldon Spiegel. Those 48 people brought in 245 transactions in 42 days and they averaged 2.66 referrals generated per person per week. That's pretty heavy.

Dean: Those are some great numbers.

Floyd: I know. That's about normal. My trainer Mary Johnson recently graduated a program with H.E.R. Realtors and 30 people did 135 listings, 174 sales, averaging 1.98 referrals per person per week over a 42-day period of time. H.E.R. Realtors, they're now kicking off their eighth program and have had more than 200 of their agents complete the program over the past year.   Mike Pallin graduated a program with RE/Max action in Chicago, same way, 0.93 transactions per person per week, 2.17 referrals per person per week. Everywhere, the same results and we're very proud of that and we can do that for any company.   Somebody one time said they became successful learning "The Wickman Way". At first I was embarrassed and confused but they spelled out the acronym S.M.A.R.T. which are the components I first brought into the real estate then I guess I can call it the Wickman Way.

Most importantly, what we do is this, our niche, we work for the client, (not the agent) and with the client and, we focus our energies on their bottom 50% of producers and turn them into the top 50%...

Dean: It's sustainable.

Floyd: Absolutely.

Dean: It tells you that when they've developed that

foundation themselves, after doing all that SMART training for a seven week period, now that's sustained.

Floyd: Absolutely, what doesn't sustain is that high degree of energy and exertion, remember they're going through a program and then you have to do all these assignments and they have to work together in these, so as far as energy and effort that seems to fall off right after graduation. But they don't need as much energy and effort and some people never succeed. 9% of the people that start the program end up out of the program. Of those 4% get struck out, but that's okay. Can't save the ones that are un-savable, but boy we can certainly do a lot for a company's bottom line. And last but not least, I think it is important that I talk about whether the program is a fit for your company because that's always a question.

Here's Exactly How to Get Started Flipping Your Company Right Side Up Risk Free...

I don't know what brokers and managers are hearing, but I'll tell you precisely how a broker puts together a Floyd Wickman Program and I call it a risk free method of determining if it's right for you and there are four simple steps. The first step is to contact my company at www.floydwickman.com and inquire about a program. What we will do is match you up with the right kind of trainer for your company. Some people like female trainers, some like male, some like ones that specialize in certain markets. Yeah, different strokes for different folks, we match them up with the right one. The next step is you get face to face with that person. They'll go in and meet with you and strategize the potential of having a program. No cost to you for them to come in. If that looks good, then we can do a leadership meeting with your managers. Let's pretend you think you want the program, you meet with the trainer and you say, "Yeah, I want this program for my company." Well, the management has to get behind it. Managers of your different offices or brokers and if it's a franchise in different areas, they may have to get behind you. We go on and we do a three hour leadership meeting and some times, each can be combined. What we do is we take the (obligation) monkey off the brokers back and we put it on the manager's back, do you want to have a program? If they say yes, then you get a free seminar with your agents, anywhere from three to four hours and it's all nuts and bolts how to. 90% of that free seminar is all how to list and sell, six ways that people can take themselves from the bottom to the top, powerful seminar, no cost to you, no fee.

If you want the program and your managers want the program, then the decision is on the agent's back to sign up for a program, then you have a program and the rest is history.

Dean: I can't think of anything fairer than that.

Floyd: First of all, brokers, they have people that they have to count on, their managers, to get behind them. Managers don't want to put pressure on their agent, so have a seminar and let the agents decide.

But only if a broker would get behind it, because they want to encourage the managers. If managers encourage the people, then there's a program. We don't want brokers paying for their people. We want people to pay for themselves.

Dean: Right. That's interesting, so they value it.

Floyd: Yeah, absolutely. I mean sometimes brokers do give incentive if you get so many listings during the program or early closing or reimburse you at something. There's lot of ways to do it, but the bottom line is we hardly ever go anywhere, get this far along and not end up with a program.

Dean: That's awesome, how quickly can somebody go from that first inquiry to actually having a program started, what kind of timeline is that?

Floyd: Well, okay, it's difficult to answer because if it's a smaller company, then I let my trainers establish all their own minimums. I even do a program myself once a year, just so my trainers can't tell me that something doesn't work. But like for me, if I went in and had a face to face, I'd want the leadership meeting immediately following that and then about five to six weeks later we have that free seminar. Now, I have some trainers that if it's local to them, if it's not a long flight, etc., etc., they can go in and do a small group and a broker can often times put a small group together in two weeks, you could begin a program. It all depends on the size of the company.

How Can a Broker Arrange for a Risk Free Seminar Type Introduction?

Dean: But it all starts once you go into www.floydwickman.com and start an inquiry.

Floyd: Exactly, just a matter of saying, I want to talk to a trainer about the program, then we'll call you, we'll talk with you and we'll help determine what are the characteristics of the trainer you're looking for.

Dean: That's great. Thanks for sharing all of this information with us Floyd. I think this is very valuable information for the brokers and managers to know their bottom producers into top producers.

Floyd: That's what we are hoping to do here. It's our passion helping make top producers out of the agents the brokers have written off as non-performers.

Here Is How to Turn Your Bottom Producers into Your Top Producers...

Most brokers know how to keep their top producers producing, and keep their business going. The real challenge, and the greatest opportunity for huge growth, is knowing how to turn around the bottom producers.

That's where we come in. We help brokers just like you grow their companies by turning the bottom producers into top producers with the Floyd Wickman Program. And it can all start in as little as six weeks. Here's how.

Step 1: We invest 60 minutes and meet with you to make sure the program is a fit for you and your culture.

Step 2: We meet with your leadership team and managers to strategize the potential of having a program.

Step 3: We take it from here and provide training with your bottom performing agents on all the fundamentals they are missing; the nuts and bolts of how to list and sell. Free of charge to you, the broker. We put the accountability on the person who matters, the producers themselves.

Now you can gain the most results for your office by turning your bottom producers into your top performers.

If you'd like us to help, just send an email to: rightsideup@floydwickman.com and we will take it from there.

About the Author

Floyd Wickman has touched the lives of millions of people from across the globe. His life story, captivating humor and ability to connect with people has made him a cultural phenomenon.

Born and raised in a rough section of Detroit, Michigan, Floyd Wickman learned all of life's lessons the hard way. Expected to fail at everything he did, he was once known in his office as the "Undertaker" because he drove prospects around until they died.

Then something happened at the lowest ebb of his life that changed him forever. He opened his mind to the secrets of success and became so successful he devoted his life to teaching others.

Today, Floyd stands at the helm of the Floyd Wickman Team, an organization that continues to produce the most results-oriented, successful training programs and systems ever created with millions of students worldwide.

Floyd Wickman is the author of eight top selling books and some of the most sought-after audio and video products available. He is the recipient of the "Platinum Award" for audio sales in excess of one million and his works are considered a "must-have" staple for personal libraries.

Floyd reached a career pinnacle when he was inducted into the National Speakers' Association Hall of Fame and earned the Council of Peer's Award of Excellence, an honor shared by legends such as Dr. Norman Vincent Peal, Zig Ziglar, Earl Nightingale and Og Mandino.

He was named by the National Association of Realtors and Realtor Magazine as one of the 25 Most Influential People in Real Estate and has spoken to more than 3,000 audiences in North America and abroad.

Floyd was one of the first to bridge the phenomenal reach of Social Media with tried-and-true Master Sales techniques to put more money in people's pockets despite economic conditions. His inspiration and teachings help people be more successful than they've ever imagined both in their careers and personal lives.

From humble beginnings to Keynote Speaker, Sales Industry Leader and Innovator – Floyd's first focus is on his students, clients and audiences. We Get by Giving — starts right here.